# After Image

Mary Turley-McGrath

# AFTER IMAGE

*After Image*

is published in 2020 by
ARLEN HOUSE
42 Grange Abbey Road
Baldoyle
Dublin 13
Ireland
Phone: 00 353 86 8360236
arlenhouse@gmail.com
arlenhouse.blogspot.com

ISBN 978–1–85132–216–9, paperback

Distributed internationally by
SYRACUSE UNIVERSITY PRESS
621 Skytop Road, Suite 110
Syracuse, NY
USA
13244–5290
Phone: 315–443–5534
Fax: 315–443–5545
supress@syr.edu
syracuseuniversitypress.syr.edu



Typesetting by Arlen House

cover image: 'Amaryllis in Blue' by Brian McDaid
is reproduced courtesy of the photographer

# Contents

*for Dan, Ruth and Hannah*

# After Image

# Tesserae

*What was, endures in imagination.*
*What is, waits for destruction.*

– Adam Zagajewski, 'Spider's Song'

## Hyacinths

The grape hyacinths in a forgotten box
beside the tree are found on Little Christmas.

The corms, half the size of an egg, rest
on a layer of compost, ready to escape;

two green shoots have already broken
the tissue paper outer coat,
the fragile strings of white root dangle.

Have we left them too late? The sticker reads:
*keep in a dark, airy place for up to fourteen weeks.*

We label their dark blue ceramic bowl, place it
on top of the storage press in the garden shed.
Should we die, someone would surely spot them.

## PRIMAVERA

February in the garden of Finca la Pescadera,
fruit and blossoms fill orange tree branches
rare as swallows in the valley two weeks ago.

You shaped this place from light brittle soil
overlooking the Genal that now meanders
fat and full after heavy winter rains;

scrub and weeds disappeared to make space
for trees – orange, lemon, mandarin, satsuma;
last spring you planted three pomegranates
grown from saplings on a friend's hacienda.

You are closer to nature's energy than anyone I know;
curator of eight acres of chaparro, acebuche, encina
that surge down the slopes of your demesne
to a hidden boundary, the Arroyo del Moro.
Here, you have created your other Devon.

## EASTER
*a photo etching by Margo McNulty*

This time, they
saw it for themselves

saw the Great Dune open
and the man in a long white robe

walk through a light that wiped all colours
from sea, sand, and even the tricolour carried

by the band leader on the way back to the town without
even a tune played on drums or bagpipes; they staggered
    home

spreading the news to a world drained of sound
    and leeched of colour,
as if the whole domain had to be reimagined, reinvented,
    repainted again.

## Moving History

1

I had nothing when I left,
only the love of good women stretching
back behind me: my mother, my aunts
and the spirit of my grandmother,
the first woman of the house.

On Good Friday 1916, she left Cloonakilleg
for a new home with her husband and sons,
a three mile journey in April sunshine.

The boys had filled two carts with chairs,
beds, table, stools and the open dresser.
The pots and crockery, brown mugs and
dinner plates were packed in tea chests.

Under a rug on the donkey trap seat
she placed the holy pictures swaddled
in strips of old sheets: the Sacred Heart,
Flight into Egypt, a small Salvador Mundi
in a Spanish-style, and a round picture
of the Holy Family.

My father carried the accordion in front
with his elder brother, both teenage lads.
The youngest of eight, aged four, toddled
at the back of the horse-drawn carts.

2

The new house had a kitchen,
parlour, dairy and three bedrooms.
When she climbed the stairs to look
out the south-facing window
she thought she was in paradise.

Next day, cattle and sheep were driven
from the old homestead to new flat fields
that spread from the main road to the river.
Four days on, news of 'trouble in Dublin'
reached them from Roscommon station.

3

Their new way of life began:
new rooms, new sheds, new land,
stone walls to build, a tillage field set
away from grazing sheep and cows.

History took its course: The Spanish Flu,
Black and Tans, Civil War, Economic War;
but they survived,
they all helped out and held together.
In time, the boys left as young men;
my father remained and married.

A new generation began with my birth.
I remember my calm, alert grandmother,
her bright, keen, blue eyes watching me.

Now, I see what was there all the time:
her life map penned out in invisible ink.
I had everything when I left.

## Murmuration

Avian sky etchings
across a winter bog

starlings in helix patterns
drawn to ancestral scores

audible harmony
aerial telepathy.

## Faces in an Exhibition

*King House, April 2016*

Slanting sun warms the 'Rise of Man',
a bronze spiral-staircase sculpture
with a solitary figure on the fifteenth step.

In the 1913 photograph of Irish Volunteers
the boyish faces are serious. Thirty-one
of them in full uniform, heads uncovered;
they await the photographer's flash, sense
the time-lapse gun barrel chill in warm hands.

The black and white picture fades emotions,
yet there is a hint of strain, evident unease.
Jonnie Gormley in the front row looks right,
wanting to leave; the unfamiliar disturbs.

Another photograph, nine years later, taken
at the workhouse the day British troops left
King House: four rows of men in Sunday suits
with hats or caps, the two officers in uniform;
only one gun to be seen –
the revolver in Luke Dempsey's hand.

There is a sense of relief on the faces, even
the occasional smile. Paddy Chapman in front,
hat at an angle, crosses his arms on the lapels
of his fine long coat. Beside him Richard Murray's
handsome eyes fix on the camera, his hands grip
the head of a young sheepdog between his knees.

Where are the other guns and uniforms now?
How many of them knew of the Ballinameen bomb
cast from concrete in a half tea chest, never used,
too heavy to be moved on the night it was needed?

And what they talked about that day was carried
in a wind song above the heads of 1916 veterans
on their way to the courthouse in the Crescent.

## One Man and his Dog

*a painting by Kate Murtagh Sheridan*

On Sundays he walks to the sea,
stands on the rocks and looks out,
he never strolls to the tideline,

just stands there and waits
for spirals and circles of sunset
on Sundays he walks to the sea.

He clasps the hurleys in his left hand,
the lead for the dog in the other,
he never strolls to the tideline

when calm evening waters drink
gold of sundown or sea mist veil,
on Sundays he walks to the sea.

He wants to toss the *sliotar,* strike
it to where he found Sean Óg, but
he never strolls to the tideline.

He dreams of playing their game
in a kingdom beyond the horizon,
on Sundays he walks to the sea,
he never strolls to the tideline.

## Painting Shylock

On evenings before Shabbat he painted you,
sitting in your counting room, hands relaxed,
the 'good book' in your left hand.

The spectacles slid down your nose as he painted.
Dressed in your black coat and hat, you balanced
the weight of the book.
When he mixed the paint, you felt sweat well up
where the beard was thickest.
You longed to take off the heavy broad-rimmed hat,
if only for a moment.

Ten evenings you spent like this until he finished
lining in every frown and knot on your forehead;
a new portrait, a wedding gift for your daughter.

## News from Stetin

My city is on the Baltic where amber comes from;
summers very good when I was a boy,
three months of sun – twenty degrees,
now, my father tell me, it is often thirty;

winters very cold when I was a boy,
many falls of snow – often minus twenty,
now, my father tell me, only one fall of snow.
Climate change, my father say, is here.

*He sighs and his blue eyes reflect morning light*
*in the taxi rear-view mirror.*

My children like it here – speak English well;
we visit my father and brothers each summer.
I like to go home but I come back to Dublin,
a lot of rain – but I don't mind.

## New Exodus

*The child presses against the mesh,*
*a wire of cold steel between her lips;*
*her hands grip squares that hold her back.*

She dreams of her home city:
the souk with fruit and spices,
almonds, oranges, figs, dates,
rolls of cloth from Pakistan,
lapis lazuli from Afghanistan,
music of zurma, oud and drum,
antics of acrobats in the square.

Now it's all gone: home, souk,
square, school, music, mosque;
friends left, grandparents dead,
blasted streets, no food, no water,
the ugly smell that made her sick.

They followed the road they never knew,
then train tracks melting towards the sky;
mother calmed the crying baby,
her eyes damp always. Father carried her,
with their extra clothes in his backpack.

*Now they are stopped by wire, soldiers and dogs;*
*men drag at the fence.*
She dreams again of her home city.

## Aspects of Colour

I remember only two colours,
deep velvet red and dust grey,

the velvet red of my city
after plane drops of cluster bombs,

the velvet red of dried blood
on children's faces, faces grey

with dust like aged goblins
in filthy shambled rooms,

toppled pillars everywhere
over trapped rotting bodies.

When I wake, I pray for the love
of God, white clouds in a blue sky.

I remember only two colours,
deep velvet red and dust grey.

## LEDWIDGE CENTENARY
*Slane Castle 2017*

All the lines are read,
the audience ambles from the room.

I move to the west window and look down
on the tree-lined path where you walked
as a kitchen boy
and thought about your brother's coughing
night after night; it frightened you awake.

You never stood in this mirrored ballroom
nor in the grand hall where now the music
of a young violinist
thrills the space between crested walls;

the half-open great door frames the trees
already dusted cinnamon at the park's end.

Outside, evening tones the air to amber
while across the lawn towards the Boyne
a white bird rises above the weir;

a dark-haired young man watches too –
*a swan,* he says, *and there on a post*
*looking over the weir, is a heron.*

We watch in the losing October light.
One circle closes, another begins.

## Blind Truth: Walk your Talk

*a carving by Adam Burthom*

Light had left my eyes
long before

the endless moment
came from the sky
in a thermal blast;

the world jolted
and through my skin
I saw heat that twisted
my very gut and sinews.

I fled deeper into my cave
to a darkness burying
fractal geometry of ruin,
debris of carbon forms

under a blood-red sun
on a snow-white peak.

## Nala

was the new wife in the village;
she would help the rains return
and crops grow. They made

love each night in their new hut
and in weeks she was with child;

when the planting season came
she sowed seeds with the others;

prayed as she dropped grains
of maize and millet into solid soil.

She could feel the child stir
in her womb, each day stronger
in the heating landscape;

the seeds took root. She prayed
as they began their fragile life
like tiny colourless ants;

he smiled at her growing belly.
In bed each night she felt his root
grow sturdy until one morning

the stalks had withered;
*like last year*, he said, kicking the clay;

the ground grew harder. One night
the baby kicked his father's back;
next morning he left.

## THE CORDOBA SCROLLS

1

From the roof of the Calahorra Tower we watch
the Guadalquivir's pale olive water carry shades
of copper and manganese from Sierra Morena
down under the arches of the Roman bridge.

Further back spreads the Great Mosque:
its minaret, arches and triangular roofs shelter
the marble prayer halls of double arches
where once more than sixty thousand prayed.

2

In the shade of the tower an artist displays
his parchments of ornate Arabic calligraphy.
We watch his elegant hand guide the brush
from right to left, draw lavish linear secrets
to inscribe our names on the pristine scrolls.

Then we find a third scroll among his exhibits;
a pattern in dark blue and yellow of the line
from Rumi: *Woman is a ray of divine light.*

3

On the bridge a trio: violin, guitar, flute, play
at the statue of St Rafael, patron of the city.
They are performing O'Carolan's Concerto,
elegant and complex in sound as Arabic script.

## LOUGH ESKE
*Lake of the Fish*

Afternoon in blue-grey light
by the lake edge of thin reeds
screening a scatter of rocks.

We walk towards the slipway
and more rocks appear,
an archipelago of hummocks
softened by moss

as everything is softened
on this mild winter's day;
trees embossed with lichen,
grey-green tufts of sponge
that thrive in pellucid air.

We could fish in the still water,
catch brown trout or sea trout,
but four pairs of mallards have
reserved the place,
keeping the peace of wild things.

# Annaghmakerrig

*... I understood*
*how anyone in darkness longs for green ...*

– Ruth Padel, 'Salon Noir'

## Return

*Your room is ready,* the housekeeper said:
midday windows flicked open and a breeze
spiralled in the staircase like a spirit memory;

ten years gone; I am back in this room again,
this green room overlooking wide lawns
and a lake that embraces the world.

Before me the days opened; each morning
the lawns exhaled where small paths curved
under trees to the summer silence

under hazel, ash and pines in an innocence
I had not found before

a mood of meditation, of rest after struggle –
to find myself in a green-blue place
where swallows called, dipped and soared;
at night herons called from lake reeds

and I knew this was as close to Heaven
as I could get; and the days went on

and someone came into my life and left
and so did others, all gifting treasures
– stories, songs, images.

I could never grasp the power of this place
in stillness, storms or moonlight;
how on mornings when nothing moved

I felt trapped as if in a painting, looking
inwards and outwards, secure in layers
of pied pigments, invisible, unheard.

## Memory

Love dreams from this place sustained me,
this room of high twin windows watching
lawn and lake, the redwood's layered bark,
cerise rhododendron blossoms glowing

the lake water changing as day changed:
in morning tangos unleashing diamonds,
afternoon shimmers from shore to shore,
evening tree shade lost in waltzing reeds;

and there was birdsong, birdsong echoes
above geomancy of swallows' flight paths
over roofs, across the lawn, under trees,
from copper beech to reedy maze.

## A Heron

rises from the fluted reeds,
flies evenly across the placid lake

like in the Egyptian creation myth
when the call of a benu bird stirred
the waters
                    and the world began
with this bizarre bird – languid,
deliberate, not even beautiful;

I imagine her first raucous call
that broke primordial silence,
a sound stored in the inner ear.

## CONTINUUM

Today I reach the lake's end
edged by April trees – alder, willow, birch,
all cluttered along the brink as if by right
to mark the end of water, to set limits.

Under the trees, a scatter of rubbish:
plastic Lucozade and Coca-Cola bottles,
Ariel boxes, part of a barbeque, a child's
navy and yellow canvas shoe, size eight.

Nature ignores these insults here;
fallen trees have regrown, ditches display
clumps of primroses and violet bouquets,
the colour the thinnest rainbow line.

A tall blackthorn spreads its white flowers,
a 'new covenant' behind the other trees.

## After Image

The lake is still the same

reflected pines in morning shadow panoramas
surpass their own reality

            we fall in love with images
from the past, images of lovers, images
of ourselves; those priceless duplicates we keep

            like newsreels in our heads:
dead fathers, mothers, lost childhoods, days at work
or play, pain or joy,
            all saved in the temporal lobe
            making our transitory selves.

## REJOICE

*Beauty growls from the fertile dark*
– Denise Levertov

To find these words now
as the world shimmers about me –

the chestnut tree already green,
fat, pink buds on the copper beech,
the lake glittering at midday –

if only we could catch and keep this,
if only we knew how;

when evening comes, it fades
with the new moon's crescent.

## Diorama

This evening I took a path to the lake's end
to find newly-minted water,

the sun on its way to setting shone a spotlight
across the wavelets making
the surface shimmer

then beamed a chaos of dappled flickering shadows
on alders, beech and birch,
like disco strobe lights

from an invisible crystal ball, dapple on dapple
with filmic circling
on the screen of trees

they could not feel it, could not see it, even then
their leaves opening, their roots in dank soil.

## THE EDGE

At the lake's end
with a branch I lever up
the shallow stones; mud water
rises, spreads and falls. I prise again
and watch another gentle, perfect resettling
as if nothing had happened, as if I did not exist.

## Before the Naming

Is this where it all went wrong
with language, with the naming of things?

So that we know tree or flower or water –
think we know them, but rarely think

of the chlorophyll miracle of trees or the map
of world weather in their rings for centuries

or stored in their hearts, old world images
that flourished before the time of dinosaurs

in the ginkgo trees with their split fan leaves
that survived extinction only in central China
but thrive again in modern cities we inhabit.

## Before Speech

These never talked – trees, water, flowers;
all speechless,

have no words, gestures, expressions,
no force can make them;

but if taken from us, we who have words
for everything and nothing would

become smaller, sadder, lifeless beings,
without these wordless things

and above our Earth space station crews
circling the planet every ninety minutes
say how beautiful it is,

see how land has been consumed by cities,
how forests have dwindled,
how ice fields on Kilimanjaro have melted.

## Shadow on Shadow

again
I watch as I do each day
the same waterscape in pure sunlight

slanting rays seem to lift the lake
as if to draw it skywards

the darker shades of trees absorb light,
consume it into themselves

stillness remains

a swan glides from her nest
in the shelter of reeds, then drifts

like a Greek letter
over an open page.

from those hidden places we forget,
put aside, withhold, until one day

a faint eclipse suddenly brings back
a face, a smile or the turn of a head

and begins this human need for union,
for a deep overlap of souls so intense
Heaven's own forces cannot destroy,

and long after the drift away is done
something else is born, the knowing
what was the need to find it,

and to find it again, somewhere else,
to find fertile dark, trust the heart
and savour what you find.

## Lake Pagoda

The afternoon is grey with bursts of sun
that cannot change the water, but near
the pagoda a crescent of reeds curves
into the lake, tall oaten stems foiled
by metal water –

like Lake Biwa in Japan
and where the chestnut trees once stood,
rows of cherry blossom unfurl to welcome
a line of saffron monks with shaven heads
who appear slowly from beyond the reeds.

If the pagoda were bigger they could enter
and pray; as it is they lay copper bowls
of cherry petals and fresh jasmine incense
at the golden Buddha's feet – then continue
in a file to the boathouse to fish for supper.

## Rhododendron and Chaffinch

This cerise electric pulse,
*a blow in,* set like a sore thumb
against the soft green lawn

each day becomes my outer heartbeat –
a thrust of morning energy and once
when the song of a chaffinch began

I remembered the racing of your heart
on the speeding birth monitor
that summer midnight when it was
only you and me against fate.

## Sands of the Well

*after Denise Levertov*

My world sleeps inside your book

each day I read your pages and find
we share the same places, but apart –

that I have a conjoined existence
with you, twenty years dead,

who wrote of herons, forests
and life beside a lake;

the yellow tulips open
on the lawn near the redwood;

a caravan from the desert dust
has already arrived.

## Swallows

They arrive today, a Sunday blessing
in a place there are no bells,
where I need no bells,

each day bringing a miracle
of faith in the divine beauty of things
in themselves, their splendid patterns

so, when two swallows skim the grass
on an afternoon when the air cools
to bring showers of hail

I wonder how long
their tiny bodies were in flight,
how they found their way back

using the code for magnetic north
and the wisdom of generations.

## Patterns

The pleated scarf you sent
surprised me with its overlapped colours,
like folded quills of birds in webbed water
of multi-coloured late autumn currents

lapis lazuli, deep blue, royal blue,
red, rust, peach, purple, grey-blue,
with a cross weave of red,
green, white and sky blue;

opened out, it makes rolling terraces
in a Japanese landscape, hides ripples
of secret dreams in folds, silken sheen
in evening sunlight, velvet of twilight.

## Before the Storm

clouds topple in as the wind rises;

at the lake's edge there is chaos –
water thrashes the sands,
the lake bed churns and wretches
and heaves from its stomach: stones,
timber, sand, reeds, buds broken
from the ash.

*It is something I can do,* the lake says:
*toss, thrash and spew out my entrails.*
*I would prefer to be quiet, motionless,*
*but I can do this too and sink your boat*
*and make you shudder at my fierceness.*
*This is me also, as sure as you are.*

## THE STORM

comes as darkness folds over the water
first, rain that turns to sleet and snow,
tiny ice flakes of light pitch against
ever-deepening blackness.

Blackness seeps in anyway, fades out
gardens, trees, lake and pagoda, until
from the window I can see only
my own stark silhouette reading
about secret streams, light speed

and old Odysseus setting out bravely
on his travels again.

The wind rises to a howl,
growls across from the pine hill,
flaps the water like a plastic sheet
but the herons, water hens and swans
are safe in shelters of matted reeds,
their necks wound round each other.

Odysseus will return, of course,
that kind always do.

## AFTER THE STORM

the rhododendron blossoms are lost;
handfuls of cerise festoon the grass
under the silver birch and spruce

and some scatter over path stones
foiled by their browns and greys;

the redwood still stands solemnly
as swallows twitter from chimneys
out of sight

and the lake sparkles
while a new breeze lures
the water from shore to shore

allows no reflection
of the pine hill, just a wide dark band
by the far bank, an obscure memory.

each morning brought the gift of light –
the sun already warming the garden;
yellow tulips and bluebells flowered
in the glory of April's ending; summer
days yet to come – the magnificent
promise of it all

along the woodland path where
banks of primroses curved their faces
to afternoon sun; frost-white candles
of the laurel hedge stretched for heat
away from shading pines and hazels;

the old crushed leaves made carpets
to the redbrick gatehouse; the collie
waited, his eyes full of old questions.

What brought me back to this place?
A gift from heaven after gruelling years,
wars, famine, bombings, even earthquakes
on the world's roof, avalanches on Everest;

yet this place is still pristine –
new born, perfect, unblemished
while the world spins on its own grit;

we have almost learned not to pollute,
not to contaminate, not to poison,
not to make deserts, and that life can
and does renew when rivers return.

as afternoon sun transforms the water,
lake diamonds gleam as if possessed

but in hours the lake returns to itself,
smooth, reflective, moving to a breeze
when it rises, shimmering, crimpling
again and again;
the calls of new swallows
rebound as they scan grass and shrubs;
their aerial chatter overflows the garden
of exotic cerise rhododendron blooms

we have learned to treasure what once
we took as given, for should we lose it,
we dread what may come instead.

## Leaving

The bank at the lake's edge is soggy.
Sliding, I balance myself

for my last pilgrimage. The water
still thrashes after rain, the breeze
drives waves forward, insistent,
always arriving.

I return to walk back by a path
on the other side of the lake,
through forest and a new clearing
at the west end

but a heavy pole set in clamps
blocks the road above a scatter
of broken glass;
signs to return the way I came.

## Squirrels in the Wild

Mother loved to talk about them,
how they scampered up the trees
of the plantation in Castle Ffrench.

We listened and were jealous –
we had never seen them but
loved her stories
of rusty tails and little paws;

today in the woods I heard
a noise in the trees and stopped,

waited to see two of them scamper
almost to the top of a beech tree
then turn to look down at me –
past and present fused.

I hold that memory fresh as when
she told us about them as children.
I retain her wonder and girlish spirit,
delight in things she relished most.

## THE LOST GARDEN

Almost ten years, a whole decade slipped
through my fingers like your amber rosary;

to count all that happened, to condense it
into pages – impossible –

so much lost, more gained. New grandchildren
to delight your memory, your name;

for me, the presence of a lost garden, terraced
plots, once full of roses, artichokes, montbretia;

now, colonies of wild flowers spread everywhere
crowd under the sundial, fallen on its numbers;

time stopped, refused to move when the gardener left.

## May Day

Last night, a full moon loitered
over the fairy fort, lured back
an old dimension to new time.

You saw a church in the woods –
it appeared between the birches,
then vanished; you searched
old maps and charts, found nothing.

Now you cannot sleep; can only hear
children's laughter from Poll na Gáire
and dream of an old lady in black
at the dead of night.

# Winter Poems

*Silence*
*deepened, deepened. The short day*
*suspended itself, endless.*

– Denise Levertov, 'Swan in Falling Snow'

## College

This winter I must search for you again
around the small cafés off Grafton Street,
or in the Dining Hall under florid faces
of eighteenth century orators in well-fitted
breeches and fur-trimmed robes.

Below them at long tables, the din rose
from the clattering cutlery of chattering students
and cocoons of lecturers in academic discussion.

That was years ago. Today, the great doors
are locked, the students gone for Christmas.
Parties will begin later. You are not here.

## The Cricket Pitch

Midday sunlight bands the cricket pitch
etching the icy swards to Nassau Street;
tree shadows rest on frosted grass; clay
cannot contain them, they lift and fade.

On my newspaper, images of Aleppo's ruins:
shelled streets where women carry baggage
and children drag sacks, quit derelict homes.
Backdrop to the exodus, a single minaret.

A figure in a blue coat at a broken window
watches them pack into waiting coaches.
Snow falls. They face winter in canvas tents.
How many will return, and when?

## THE YELLOW TREE

Nine years on, the same light above Westland Row;
clouds drape like plumes of thought over this city
dreaming about itself, over the silent cricket pitch
lined with trees already changed, over leaves piled
in heaps by diligent gardeners.

I search for a chestnut burr to place in your hand.
Once we gathered burrs, felt the cream velvet
inside their thorny skin on those last evenings,
I wonder now if they were real or dream.

The golden globe at the library reveals dark gashes,
its centre exposes struts holding it together, beams
keeping the core at bay. But the yellow tree is gone.

I scan the avenue for its honey glow – there is nothing;
only an empty space where crab apples dot the grass.

## In Black and White

*The Douglas Hyde Gallery*

You survived the Great War and with one arm
Josef Sudek you made photographs of Prague
with old cameras left in the studio you bought.

The film needed was almost impossible to find.
You wiped developed negatives, re-used films.

How often did you arrange cameras, haul tripods
up flights of stairs, across roofs of tall buildings,
to capture a crisp image of St Vitus Cathedral?

You trekked fields and wasteland outside the city,
saw ruins, gas tanks, mines – legacy of another war.

On summer evenings you watched raindrops form
on moveless branches in Otto Rothmayer's garden.
You waited for those transparent pearls,
longed for them passively as for a muse.

## The Lost Café

*One shot or two*? she asks, her eyes dark as Polish forests;
eyes like yours, just like yours

and I remember that winter café years ago
where we escaped from frozen crowded streets

you were always late from study in the Berkeley
so I waited, immersed in coffee aromas,

then you'd arrive, full of new ideas and connections
that exploded like summer cocktails between us

those evenings I forgot to savour the Arabica from
high Columbian plantations where pickers harvested
cherries, two coffee beans in each; wild parrot cries
and calls of meandering geese split their silent work.

*One shot or two*? she asks again.
*Two*, I say, not knowing why.

## The House

This is the house I may die in –
it looks innocent enough, quite unperturbed
by the notions I cast on it. The redbrick facade
is flat and introverted like those facades of tall
houses in postcards you sent me from Quebec;
flatness that allows gusts of wind move round
without a chance to test high elegant windows,
whose complex sash systems lie hidden behind
panelled shutters like the insides of old clocks.

Ten granite steps lead to a Prussian blue door;
the knocker, a lion's head like a brass Cerberus
with a scowl, jolting the hearts of timid callers.
Maybe if I knock gently he will not receive me;
even if he does not, it is all a question of time,
the toss of that coin I will never hold.

## An Old Friend

You welcome me, as you always do,
to your old world kitchen where the ceiling
is low above us and the Aga sends the hiss
of oozing mince pies across scrubbed tiles.
I sit near the fridge, my body slow to alter
after chilly rambles through dreary streets.

You have baked a special cake in my honour:
a sponge, with generous amounts of butter,
and flakes of grated courgettes like the chips
of lemon peel my mother put in treacle cake.

We find the picture of your uncle's farmhouse
in the For Sale section of the weekend paper.
It stands proudly overlooking Meenmore Bay,
its clock tower and walls date to 1787.

## Evening

Light wilts to a miasma between day and night,
bare apple tree branches ingest the blackness.
Three small apples are wedged in the tree forks,
now, winter's captives, their pale green wanes.

You have planted a golden bamboo
at the garden's end; it brings good luck you say.

Darkness comes with rain, and the apples fade
giving way to lurid lights from Christmas trees,
those electric miracles charging our brains
with signals to fight darkness in our souls.

The silver gates we entered have led nowhere;
parents flee burning cities, carry their children;
one man grasps his father by the hand;
this new age Aeneas has no home.

## Acknowledgements

Thanks are due to the editors of the following journals and anthologies in which some of these poems, or versions of them, have appeared: *Strokestown International Poetry Festival Anthology* (2018); *Reading the Future: New Writing from Ireland* (2018); *New Roscommon Writing Anthology* (2018); *Cyphers* 82; *Boyne Berries* (2017); *Washing Windows Irish Women Write Poetry* (2017); *An Image: A Poem* (Roscommon County Council, 2017*); Centenary in Reflection Anthology* (Siarsceal, 2016)

I would also like to thank the director and staff of the Tyrone Guthrie Centre, Annaghmakerrig where many of these poems were written during a residency awarded to me as winner of the Trócaire/Poetry Ireland Competition 2014.

My thanks to all in Poetry Ireland, and to my family for their help and support over the years.

## About the Author

Mary Turley-McGrath is from Mount Talbot on the Galway/Roscommon border; she now lives in Letterkenny. She holds an M.Phil in Creative Writing from Trinity College, Dublin and has published three collections of poetry: *New Grass under Snow* (Summer Palace Press, 2003), *Forget the Lake* (Arlen House, 2013), and *Other Routes* (Arlen House, 2016).

Mary is the winner of a number of national awards: Trócaire/Poetry Ireland Award, Francis Ledwidge Award and the Annie Deeny Award through the Arts Council of Northern Ireland and the Arts Council/An Comhairle Ealaíon. Her work has also been shortlisted in many competitions, including Cúirt and the Single Poem Competition at Listowel Writers' Week.

Her poems have been published in numerous anthologies and in journals and newspapers including *Poetry Ireland Review* and *The Irish Times*. Her work has been broadcast on RTÉ1's *Sunday Miscellany* and she has given readings at Strokestown International Poetry Festival, Shorelines Poetry Festival, Clifden Arts Festival, Poetry Ireland and in the United Arts Club, Dublin.

*After Image* is her fourth collection.